P9-DGV-623

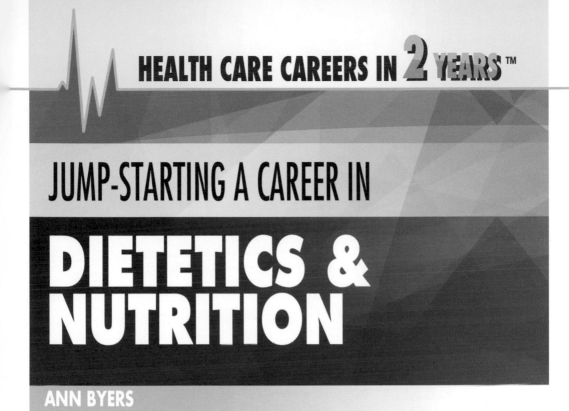

HEALTH CARE CAREERS IN 2 YEARS ™

JUMP-STARTING A CAREER IN

DIETETICS & NUTRITION

ANN BYERS

ROSEN
PUBLISHING®

New York

Published in 2014 by The Rosen Publishing Group, Inc.
29 East 21st Street, New York, NY 10010

Copyright © 2014 by The Rosen Publishing Group, Inc.

First Edition

All rights reserved. No part of this book may be reproduced in any form without permission in writing from the publisher, except by a reviewer.

Library of Congress Cataloging-in-Publication Data

Byers, Ann.
Jump-starting a career in dietetics and nutrition/Ann Byers.—First edition.
    pages cm.—(Health care careers in 2 years)
Includes bibliographical references and index.
ISBN 978-1-4777-1691-5 (library binding)
1. Dietitians—Vocational guidance. 2. Nutritionists—Vocational guidance. 3. Nutrition counseling—Vocational guidance. I. Title.
RM218.B94 2014
613.2023—dc23

2013012405

Manufactured in Malaysia

CPSIA Compliance Information: Batch #W14YA: For further information, contact Rosen Publishing, New York, New York, at 1-800-237-9932.

CONTENTS

INTRODUCTION

Domenica Toscani knew that obtaining an associate of arts degree was just the first step in getting the job she wanted; she knew she'd have to have more than a good education. So while she was in school, she interned with a dietitian so that she could get hands-on experience and meet people in the field. She went to conferences for dietetic professionals so that she could form a wider network. She shadowed one of her professors who worked as a clinical dietitian in a long-term care facility. After she received her certification as a registered dietitian technician (DTR), she was hired by that facility.

After she landed the job as a dietitian technician, Toscani kept looking for more opportunities to do exactly what she wanted. The field of dietetics and nutrition has so many different career paths, and she wanted to explore more of them. She volunteered with a nonprofit organization as a nutrition educator. Eventually, that organization offered her a position as an evaluations consultant. That meant she not only taught but also conducted focus groups and other research to measure how much students learned and applied after attending the organization's nutrition education classes. She also maintains a food and

High school students listen to an instructor in a nutrition and wellness class. They learn how their choices of food and activities affect their health.

nutrition Web site on which she publishes recipes, articles, and links that promote healthy eating.

Her work is quite varied. Some of it is clinical: she assesses the health status of individual clients. Some of it is education and counseling, teaching groups or working one-on-one. Some is study: compiling information, designing lesson plans, figuring out the nutritional content of foods, and writing a blog. Some of her time is spent creating and tasting healthy dishes. She works some in an office, some at her clients' sites, and some from home.

Toscani could take the next step, getting more education and becoming a registered dietitian, and some day she might. But right now, she loves inspiring people to make good lifestyle choices, helping them learn how to improve their health, and watching them make simple changes that yield long-term results. She feels good because she is contributing toward a solution to the national obesity problem. Right now, she is very happy as a dietitian technician.

Chapter 1

THE FIELD

The dietetics profession in the United States is not quite one hundred years old. Even though ancient health care practitioners understood the importance of food to health, nutrition was not recognized as a medical science in America until the beginning of the twentieth century. In 1917, when World War I threatened worldwide food shortages, a group of women formed the American Dietetic Association (now the Academy of Nutrition and Dietetics). Their purpose was to conserve the country's food supply and improve the way people ate. A year later, the U.S. Army set up a Food and Nutrition Division to make sure soldiers had healthy diets. In 1919, with the war over and hospitals treating wounded veterans, the government recognized that diet was important in helping the veterans recover from malnutrition and other ailments. The Public Health Service began hiring dietitians as part of the medical teams in its hospitals.

Nutrition and Dietetics: Subtle Differences

People often use the terms "nutrition" and "dietetics" interchangeably, but they are actually slightly different. Nutrition is the science of foods and how the body uses them. It is the study of food composition and the effect of the various components of food on the body. Dietetics is the application of the principles of nutrition to health. In other words, nutrition is about the chemistry and physiology of foods and digestion, and dietetics is about using that information. Both nutritionists and dietitians work to help people get or stay healthy, but they do so in different ways. Generally, nutritionists tend to emphasize natural remedies and supplements. Many dietitians also use natural substances in their nutrition therapy along with traditional approaches.

A dietetic intern takes high school students on a field trip to a grocery store to help them learn how to read food labels and recognize healthy foods.

Nutritionists focus on wellness, on preventing health problems. They teach people how to adjust their diets, encourage them to exercise, and explain the value of nutritional supplements. They work with people with chronic conditions—problems that persist for some time—such as allergies, diabetes, and being overweight. Nutritionists do not try to cure people; they help them manage and improve their conditions and keep them from growing into bigger problems.

Dietitians are concerned with illness. Their patients generally have acute issues—that is, conditions that are serious and need immediate attention, perhaps heart disease, kidney failure, or something that requires surgery. Dietitians determine what foods will help them improve and what foods will hinder their progress. They use diet as part of treatment for the specific problem. Often a dietitian is also a nutritionist, but a nutritionist is not a dietitian.

In short, nutritionists emphasize wellness and dietitians concentrate on illness. Nutritionists prevent and manage problems; dietitians help cure them. Nutritionists counsel; dietitians treat. Nutritionists deal with ongoing conditions and dietitians deal with pressing problems. In actual practice, however, the jobs of nutritionists and dietitians often overlap, blurring the distinction between the two professions. The real difference is in their training and certification.

Licensing, Certification, and Credentialing

Dietitians and nutritionists study many of the same subjects in school. Students in both fields take classes in microbiology, chemistry, anatomy, and physiology. They study nutrition assessment—how to evaluate a person's nutritional state and needs. They also learn about nutrition therapy—how to use foods to change a patient's physical condition. This means that nutritionists and dietitians who attend schools recognized by professional associations have the same or very similar educations; they know the same information. They have many of the same skills, but they have different proofs of what they know and can do.

People in the nutrition field can prove their ability at three different levels: licensing, certification, and credentialing. A license is given by a government body, usually a state. It is basically permission to practice an occupation. Forty-seven states—all except Arizona, California, and Colorado—require people to obtain a state license in order to give nutrition advice. The standards for getting a license differ from one state to another. Therefore, some people who call themselves nutritionists have master's degrees and some have little or no training at all.

The next level is certification. A certificate is given by an association, and it attests that a person has met the standards set by the association. In an attempt to gain recognition and support for their profession, some nutritionists have joined together, forming associations, and these associations give tests and issue certificates. But the certificates are only as good as the issuing group, and there is no group that everyone accepts—no nationally recognized association—that certifies nutritionists.

The highest level of proof of a person's knowledge and skill to perform a job is credentialing. It is a stamp of approval from an organization that everyone in the field agrees has the highest expertise and authority. In the field

DIETETIC TECHNICIAN: MULTITASKER

As a registered dietetic technician, Marie Miller wears many hats. Her job at a Veterans Administration hospital allows her to practice her clinical skills. She assesses patients' nutritional status and talks with them about what they need to do to improve. She teaches classes to groups of patients. She is also an administrator, supervising DT interns and students accumulating their practice hours to become DTRs. She plans special events for the hospital that have to do with nutrition.

In addition, Miller works for a medical supply company that makes pumps for people, mostly children, who need to be fed through a tube inserted into the intestine. She delivers the pumps to her patients' hospitals or homes, keeps them in working order, and teaches patients and their parents how to use them. Whether she is working with an elderly veteran or a small infant, teaching a large class or consulting at the bedside of one child, Miller finds the many facets of her job as a dietetic technician exciting and rewarding.

of nutrition, that organization is the Academy of Nutrition and Dietetics. For almost one hundred years, this agency has set high standards for the nation's dietitians, awarding both certificates and credentials. However, it awards these only to dietitians, not to nutritionists.

Dietitian and Dietetic Technician

The Academy of Nutrition and Dietetics grants two credentials: registered dietitian (RD) and dietetic technician, registered (DTR). Both credentials have three types of requirements: education, practice, and testing. To obtain a credential, a person must have a specified level of education, must have hands-on practice under the supervision of an expert, and must pass a standardized test.

The minimum requirements for the dietetic technician credential are an associate of arts (A.A.) or an associate of science (A.S.) degree from an accredited college or university, the completion of 450 hours of supervised practice, and a passing score on the exam. Most students can earn their A.S. degree in 2 years and 450 practice hours within 3 months. So it is possible to become a DTR within two or three years of graduating from high school. A DTR has less power and less responsibility than a registered dietitian, but dietetic technician is a professional position in the medical field with a good salary.

The requirements for an RD credential are higher: a bachelor of science (B.S.) degree from an accredited school, at least 1,200 hours of supervised practice, and passing a more difficult test. The Academy of Nutrition and Dietetics offers two ways for people to get the required amount of practice. They can enroll in a coordinated program, which incorporates the 1,200 practice hours into the 4-year B.S. degree program. Or they can earn their B.S. in an approved four-year didactic program, which has classroom coursework only, and then get the practice hours in an internship. A dietetic internship usually lasts for eight to twenty-four months, and most interns receive no pay.

The two-year pathway to a DTR credential is a good career choice. It opens doors to a variety of very rewarding job possibilities. It also lays the foundation for further education and practice that will result in an RD credential, if desired. Many RDs go on to get master's or doctoral degrees that give them even more career choices.

Types of Work

Most of the career choices in the field of nutrition and dietetics can be divided into three broad categories: clinical, public health, and food service. The supervised practice required for certification includes hours in all three areas. "Clinical" means anything having to do with observing and treating patients who are sick. Public health is the medical field concerned with prevention, rather than treatment, of disease. Nutritionists and dietitians in food service oversee the way the food in big operations is selected, prepared, and served.

Each of these three areas has a number of possible career paths: practitioner, educator, researcher, administrator, and consultant. Some people work in more than one area at the same time, such as clinical practitioner

This nutritionist is conducting a class on nutrition at a school for chefs. Nutritionist and chef are both careers that can begin within two years of high school graduation.

and public health educator or food service administrator and public health researcher. Although these are the main divisions in the nutrition field, there are jobs that are hard to fit into one of these categories. Opportunities in dietetics and nutrition are indeed vast and varied.

Chapter 2

Clinical Nutrition and Dietetics

The majority of dietitians are in clinical practice. They work directly with patients in hospitals, clinics, doctors' groups, and short- and long-term care facilities such as rehabilitation and nursing homes. In clinical practice, dietitians use nutrition therapy to treat patients who are ill. The nutrition therapy is, of course, only part of any patient's treatment. RDs and DTRs in these settings are members of medical teams that may include physicians, surgeons, nurses, therapists, and other health care professionals. Clinical dietitians evaluate patients' nutritional needs, create meals and dietary plans that meet those needs, explain the plans to the patients, and check on the patients to see how well the treatment is being followed and how well it is working. Each of these responsibilities involves a number of tasks. An RD can perform all the tasks; a DTR can perform many of them and can assist the RD in others.

Assessing Nutritional Needs

Nutritional evaluation involves more than deciding whether a patient is getting enough to eat. Dietitians want

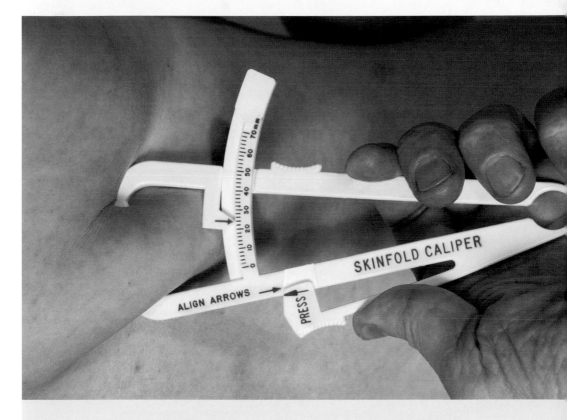

A person's weight is made up of muscle and fluids as well as fat. Skinfold calipers enable dietitians to measure body fat.

to know if patients are getting the right amount, the right kinds, and the right balance of nutrients for their particular conditions. The nutritional needs of a young woman who is pregnant are different from those of a middle-aged factory worker with heart disease. Dietitians evaluate their patients' nutritional status in four ways: with measurements and through clinical, dietary, and lab assessments.

RDs and DTRs can get an idea of patients' general status by comparing their physical measurements against

EATING FOR PERFORMANCE

Lori Tubbs is not only a registered dietitian; she is also an athlete. She has competed in thirty-eight marathons, in triathlons, and in other sporting events. Her interest in athletics led her to sports dietetics and to a job working as a civilian with the U.S. Navy. She is a dietitian for the Navy SEALs (SEa, Air, Land teams). The SEALs are not only top-notch warriors; they are also extraordinary athletes. Tubbs applies her knowledge of sports nutrition to help the SEALs maintain the fitness, energy, and sharpness they need to meet the high physical, mental, and emotional demands of their jobs.

Tubbs is part of a medical team that keeps the SEALs ready for extreme action. She believes that 60 percent of their performance is determined by what they eat. Even though she trains them in healthy food choices, they are often in places where the best foods are not easily available. So Tubbs travels with her team to their training and operations sites, seeing what foods she can find there, and creating meal plans. The meals are designed not for mere fitness, but for performance. They have to be tailored to the specific assignment; temperature, weather, altitude, physical exertion—all have a bearing on nutritional requirements. All are part of the calculations of a sports dietitian working with Navy SEALs.

established standards. They measure height and weight; the thickness of folds of skin; the circumference of a baby's head; and the distance around an arm, chest, waist, and hips. These measurements give them a starting place, but they don't identify specific problems.

A physical examination can alert the dietitian to something specific. The hair, skin, eyes, fingernails, and mouth, for example, have clues to the possibility that certain nutrients are missing. Swelling, poor reflexes, and tenderness can alert the examiner to probe further. The physical exam, combined with a health history, is a clinical tool.

After the clinical assessment, the patient is given a thorough dietary assessment. The patient reports everything eaten in the last twenty-four hours and fills out a questionnaire about food habits. A skilled dietitian interviews the patient to get a good idea of eating patterns.

Lab tests also provide vital information. Some nutrients— or signs of their absence—show up in the blood and urine. Dietitians might not administer the tests, but they interpret the results. They have to consider factors other than diet that may affect the results: medications, water intake, and overall physical and psychological conditions. They recommend nutrition therapy—an eating plan that will restore the patient to nutritional balance so that the body can deal with other health issues.

Preparing and Monitoring Dietary Plans

When creating an eating plan, dietitians start with recognized guidelines for healthy meals. Then they make adjustments for the needs and conditions of their patients. They may have to add calories or specific nutrients, eliminate salts or sugars, add fiber, or reduce liquids. They may order that a patient's food be soft, chopped fine, or pureed. They decide how much of what foods their patients can have and when they can have them.

They know that patients are much more likely to comply with nutrition therapy if their food looks appetizing and tastes good. So some RDs and DTRs experiment with recipes. Some of their patients may need to continue with their new diets when they go home from the hospital, so the dietitians need to make sure the eating plan uses foods that the patients can purchase and prepare for themselves at home.

Dietitians in hospitals make rounds to see their patients, just as other medical professionals do. They check to see if the patients' progress toward healing or lack of progress requires

Community health is concerned with helping people stay well. This public health dietitian helps a senior citizen assess his nutritional intake.

adjustments to the dietary plans. They review their patients' records and check their lab work. The job requires people skills, for dietitians work not only with their patients, but also with their patients' families and with doctors, nurses, and a variety of technicians. In nursing homes, they work with a number of nonmedical personnel, such as social workers, activities directors, and kitchen staff.

Counseling and Educating

Some of their work requires explaining and teaching. Patients want to know why they are being given or denied certain foods and how a new diet will help them. They and their families want to understand how to develop and maintain new eating habits at home. Dietitians explain how different foods affect their patients' conditions and why they need to pay attention to how they select and prepare foods.

They also teach classes in the hospital or clinic. They may offer general nutrition classes to all interested patients, or they may conduct sessions that are helpful for people dealing with particular conditions. They may hold cooking classes, encouraging people to make the dietary changes they recommend. They also provide training to nurses and other medical professionals on new developments in the field of nutrition.

As in any medical or science field, knowledge about nutrition evolves. Research is ongoing and new information is learned all the time. Guidelines are updated. Dietitians have to stay on top of the latest advances. To keep their credentials current, DTRs must have fifty hours of education every five years and RDs seventy-five hours. They also read nutrition journals and go to conferences to stay up on what is happening in the field.

Nutrition is about not only what foods a person eats but also how much. This dietitian is demonstrating how much of different foods make up a portion.

Clinical Specialties

All of the new information is making the field more complex. That means it is possible for a dietitian or a dietetic technician to specialize in one particular area of practice. Some work primarily with diabetic patients, heart patients, newborns, or people undergoing bariatric (weight loss) surgery. The Academy of Nutrition and Dietetics offers certification in five different specialties: sports dietetics and pediatric (child), renal (kidney), gerontological (old age), and oncology (cancer) nutrition. To receive certification in one of these specialties, a person must have been an RD for at least two years,

Thirteen college football programs have registered dietitians on staff. This University of Nebraska athlete is choosing food from a training table prepared by a sports dietitian.

accumulated two thousand hours of experience in the specialty area, and passed a rigorous test demonstrating competence in the specific area. Dietitians with specialist certifications have to take the qualifying test every five years to maintain their certification.

Some dietitians want to specialize in areas for which the Academy of Nutrition and Dietetics has no certification. They can obtain certification from other recognized professional groups. For example, the National Board of Nutrition Support grants certification to dietitians who have expertise at providing nutrition through feeding tubes and IVs. The American Association of Diabetes Educators offers a certificate for the specialty of diabetes educator. The possibilities for clinical dietetics are vast, and anyone can begin with a two-year program for dietetic technicians.

Chapter 3

Community Nutrition and Dietetics

ommunity health, or public health, is the branch of health care that is responsible for making sure everyone in a community has the information and resources they need to maintain good health. Public health professionals look at the conditions of a community that relate to health. They examine the water supply, cleanliness, air quality, and number of hospitals and medical offices. They consider social and economic conditions: where are the medical facilities located? Do people have transportation to get to them? Can they afford to go to the doctor? Do they know how to prevent the spread of common diseases? Do they know what foods are good for them and can they afford those foods? Public health professionals assess the needs that are in the community and decide which issues are the most pressing. They assemble teams to address the problems.

The teams consist of a variety of health care and social service providers: doctors, nurses, dentists, dental hygienists, and social workers. Because health is directly

A community health dietitian conducts training outreach, discussing ways to overcome the challenges of choosing healthy foods and sensible portions when eating at restaurants.

related to diet, many public health teams also include nutritionists.

Nutritionists

The term "nutritionist" is challenging to define. Generally, nutritionists follow the same guidelines as dietitians, but they tend to emphasize natural remedies and supplements. Many dietitians are also nutritionists; they use natural substances and food supplements in their nutrition therapy along with traditional approaches. The problem in defining nutritionist is that there are no nationally recognized standards for the profession. Many people who use the title "nutritionist" have degrees—associate's or bachelor's—in nutrition science. But others do not. People can receive certificates that show they are nutritionists, but remember: a certificate is only as good as the organization that issues it, and different organizations have different standards.

For example, consider the criteria of four separate organizations that issue certificates for sports or fitness nutritionists. The International Sports Science Association has a brief course and a test. The National Association of Sports Nutrition requires people to take an online course and attend a seminar. The American Sports and Fitness Association has an online test, and the American Fitness Professionals and Associates requires an online course. Some vocational schools also grant a sports nutrition certificate for meeting their criteria. No wonder it is hard to say what makes someone a nutritionist!

Some professionals are trying to clear up the confusion so that nutritionists are recognized as valid health practitioners. A number joined together to form the International and American Associations of Clinical Nutritionists (IAACN). This is a nonprofit organization whose members practice nutrition therapy in different health care fields. The IAACN established criteria for the profession of clinical nutritionist in 1991. Its standards are high: at least a bachelor's degree, additional classes in nutrition after the degree, and passing a difficult test. The organization, founded almost seventy-five years later than the Academy of Nutrition and Dietetics, is slowly gaining acceptance in the medical community for the position of certified clinical nutritionist.

Clinical nutritionists often work in community health settings. Some public health facilities employ registered dietitians, including RDs with master's and doctoral degrees, but they also need nutritionists. Many also use DTRs and nutritionists who do not have bachelor's degrees. Community health settings are great for people just starting out in nutrition science.

Working in a Clinic

The most common public health setting is the community health center. Community health centers are clinics that provide free or low-cost health care. They may be public (government-operated) or private, but they are often supported by funding from a local, state, or federal government agency. They usually offer both preventive care and primary care, or basic medical care. Nutritionists and dietitians at health centers give three types of services: assessments, counseling, and education.

Doctors, nurses, and other medical professionals generally evaluate people as they come into the clinic. If any patients have complaints or conditions that are directly related to diet, they are directed to a nutritionist. The community health nutritionist assesses patients' physical condition the same way as the clinical dietitian: making a physical examination, taking various

A nutritionist teaches people in a community center how to prepare winter squash. The nutrition and exercise program is part of the center's effort to combat obesity and disease.

measurements, asking questions, and looking at the results of laboratory tests.

Once nutritionists know their patients' status, they counsel them. They explain how their eating affects their bodies, and they advise them on good eating habits. They develop diet plans tailored to the needs and resources of each patient. If patients have chronic conditions, they make appointments to see the patients regularly to keep them on track with their nutrition plans.

COMMUNITY NUTRITIONIST

When Mary was in college, she worked as a dietary aide in a nursing home. She was studying dietetics and wanted to get a feel for the career. She worked her way up from aide to cook supervisor. When she got her B.A. degree, she chose not to take the test for the registered dietitian credential. Instead, she got a job as a community nutritionist with an organization that serves women and children. The organization receives money from the federal government to provide food and nutrition education and support to the women. When her clients come in for their regular appointments, Mary weighs and measures the children so that she can judge how healthy they are. Many of the women she sees have poor eating habits. Mary encourages them to adopt new, better diets. She explains to their mothers how giving their children certain foods will make them healthier. Some of the women cannot afford the milk, cheese, fruits, and vegetables that Mary suggests, but she is able to help them obtain these foods. Everyone does not follow her advice, but many do. Mary is making a difference in the health of her community, one family at a time.

Counseling is a one-on-one activity, and nutritionists also provide education. They collect the latest information available on some of the conditions that they see in the clinics: diabetes, heart problems, high blood pressure, eating disorders, and obesity, for example. These conditions are greatly affected by diet. Nutritionists conduct classes for the general public and distribute materials explaining how wise food and exercise choices can keep these problems under control.

Working in a Food Program

Community nutrition programs also have good opportunities for nutrition professionals with two-year degrees or less. Nutrition assistance programs provide food and nutrition counseling to people who are at risk of not having healthy food. The groups in a community most likely to need food assistance are children in low-income families, low-income women who are pregnant or new mothers, and the elderly who may have difficulty shopping or cooking. Some food programs provide healthy snacks or meals for children on weekends and in the summer when they cannot get breakfast or lunch at school. Some deliver ready-cooked meals to seniors in their homes or at recreation centers. Some soup kitchen–type programs offer meals to anyone in the community in need. One of the largest and most well-known community nutrition programs is the

Some college nutrition programs offer free classes and workshops to any interested group in their communities. This nutrition educator is prepared to explain the benefits of a healthy diet.

Women, Infants, and Children Supplemental Nutrition Program, known as WIC.

Nutritionists in WIC and other community nutrition programs provide the same types of services as they do in public health centers: assessments, counseling, and education. In addition, they provide either food or vouchers with which their clients can purchase the nutritious foods they need. They also refer clients to other service providers if they have additional health, welfare, or social service needs.

Besides working with clients, nutritionists in some food programs also work with food suppliers. They have to make sure the meals are wholesome, meeting nutritional guidelines. Some programs distribute food at more than one location, such as community centers, schools, and churches. Nutritionists must visit the different sites.

Community nutritionists often do community outreach. They set up events or go to places where people gather and tell them about the services of the clinics or food programs. They help people sign up for services they might need. They make presentations and distribute literature. A community nutritionist is part health care worker, part social worker, part teacher, and part administrator. Public health nutrition is a good career choice for someone who likes people and wants variety in a job.

Chapter 4

Food Service Systems

C linical and community dietitians and nutritionists work primarily with people. The third major category of work in the nutrition field, food service systems, involves working mainly with foods. A food service system is a big operation that feeds a large number of people. Hospitals and nursing homes have food service systems. So do schools, military bases, and prisons. Hotels, restaurants, and cafeterias have food systems, as do airlines and cruise ships.

There are four different types of food service systems: conventional, centralized, ready-prepared, and assembly-serve. Many facilities use a combination of two or more of the four. In conventional food service, the food is served right after it is cooked at the same location where it is prepared. Restaurants and nursing homes use conventional food service systems. Many school breakfast and lunch programs are conventional systems.

Some school districts, however, use a centralized approach. Food for several schools is prepared in one kitchen and then transported to the kitchens of the schools. At the schools, the food is reheated if necessary and served. Some restaurant chains use a centralized kitchen for some of their items, such as breads and other bakery goods.

In the ready-prepared system, meals are not served immediately after preparation; they are frozen or refrigerated and reheated later. Food preparation is completely separate from food service. Large batches of stews, soups, and sauces can be made and stored for serving days or weeks later. This system is especially useful for very large operations, such as hospitals and prisons.

In the assembly-serve system, ready-to-eat food items are purchased, heated, and put together to make meals. This system is the basis of many fast-food menus. Each one of these four types of systems has several points at which knowledge of nutrition is critical. Like the other areas in the nutrition field, food service systems offer a variety of career opportunities.

This lieutenant commander is a nutritionist who manages a nutrition program for the U.S. Navy. She offers advice and suggestions about foods that keep navy fighters physically fit.

Food Service Manager

The person in charge of the entire system is the food service manager. That person oversees the people directly responsible for each part of the system. Others may plan the menus, select the foods, purchase the ingredients, prepare the meals, and serve customers, but the managers need to make sure all those processes are done well. Sometimes that means performing some of the tasks themselves. They have to see not only that the foods are nutritious, but also that they are safe. Food service managers are concerned not only with the actual food items,

A chef *(left)* and a food service manager *(right)* talk together after a class on making healthier meals for schoolchildren. People in the food service industry must frequently update their knowledge and skills.

but also with the kitchen's equipment, sanitation procedures, and storage facilities.

Dietitians, both RDs and DTRs, and nutritionists are well
suited to be food service managers. They can analyze the
nutritional content of the meals and the effects of the
conditions under which they are prepared and served.
They have the scientific knowledge to set and maintain
quality standards for the foods and the kitchen. When
some customers request special meals because of dietary
needs or preferences, dietitians and nutritionists can
accommodate them. Although some employers, particularly those in medical facilities, require their food service
managers to be dietitians, many do not.

The job of food service systems manager is as much
about managing as it is about food. It often entails hiring
and scheduling workers, ordering and purchasing supplies, scheduling deliveries, handling budgets and
payrolls, and other administrative tasks. Managers must
have some understanding of food nutrition and safety but
not always as much education as credentialed dietitians.
The Association of Nutrition and Foodservice
Professionals has been certifying people in this field for
more than fifty years. The nationally recognized organization offers two certificates: certified dietary manager and
certified food protection professional. People do not need
a college degree to obtain one of these certifications, but
they do need to be knowledgeable about a number of
items. They must pass a two-hundred-item test showing
they are competent in four areas: nutrition, management
of food service, sanitation, and management of human
resources.

Nutrition Assistant

Lower-level jobs in food service systems are often filled by people with little or no formal education beyond high school. These positions go by several titles: nutrition assistant, nutrition services associate, nutrition clerk, nutrition services technician, and nutrition support associate. Often these are fancy titles for food servers or dishwashers. People in these jobs perform such tasks as receiving and shelving food items and supplies or cleaning and sanitizing dishes and equipment. They help cook the food or serve customers. In a cafeteria, nutrition assistants serve customers and keep the self-serve areas clean and stocked. In a school or daycare feeding program, some assistants transport food from a central kitchen to satellite locations; others put the prepared foods on plates, paying attention to portion size. Food service nutrition assistants in

Washing dishes does not require great skill but is very important in keeping foods safe. Performing such an entry-level task well can lead to more responsible and better paying positions.

DIETETIC TECHNICIAN AND PERSONAL CHEF

Studying dietetics enabled Thomas Carrig to combine his love of cooking with his interest in science. Before becoming a DTR, he was an industrial chemist. Once he had his credential, he worked as a chef in large kitchens where he had to plan his menus according to specific nutrition guidelines. Now he has his own business: he is a personal chef specializing in healthy meals. He cooks for families, and many of his clients have medical conditions that require careful attention to diet.

Chef Thomas begins his work in the evening, planning what he will cook the next day and making a shopping list. In the morning, he purchases what he needs. That way, his ingredients are as fresh as possible. Everything he needs for preparing the meals is in his car—from pots and pans to spoons and towels. He cooks at his clients' homes. For some, he prepares one or two complete meals for the entire family, and for others he might cook a week's worth. He boxes the meals, labels them, and repacks his "kitchen in a car." Except for the delicious foods in their refrigerators, his clients would not even know that he has spent three to six hours in their kitchens.

The job is the perfect blend of science, cook-ing, and creativity for Carrig. Some of his clients are on very strict diets, and he knows the nutrition content of foods. He can turn the most restrictive of ingredients into a delicious and nutritious feast.

hospitals or homes for the elderly assemble patient food trays and load the trays on delivery carts, making sure the right meals go to the right rooms. Sometimes they feed patients or residents who need such help.

These kinds of jobs may not require much in the way of nutrition skills, but they are essential to the smooth operation of a food service system. Doing this kind of work gives people experience in the nutrition field— experience that increases their knowledge, improves their skills, and enables them to advance to more responsible positions. They are good entry-level posi-tions. Many food service managers and dietitians begin their nutrition careers as some type of nutrition assistant.

Culinary Jobs

A critical part of any food service system is the culinary area: the kitchen. Two critical jobs are those of cook and chef. People often interchange these two words, but they are actually two different positions. Cooks prepare food; chefs decide how the cooks will prepare it. A chef over-sees the work of several cooks. Food service systems generally employ a number of cooks, and the chef is in charge of all of them.

People do not always think of culinary jobs as belonging to the nutrition profession. That is because chefs and nutritionists have different perspectives on food. Chefs and cooks focus on food's taste; nutritionists are concerned with food's health value. Because health has become a major concern for so many people, workers in

A student in a high school culinary arts program uses her knowledge of food preparation, nutrition, and food safety to prepare a meal for a meeting at the school.

the culinary trades are beginning to incorporate nutrition science into their art, and nutritionists and dietitians are starting to apply their knowledge to cooking.

Some culinary jobs do not require a high school education: food preparation worker, baker, and cook. It is possible for exceptionally talented cooks to work their way up from one of these entry-level, lower-paying positions to the position of head cook or chef. But most chefs learn the fundamentals of their trade in a culinary school or a culinary department of a college or university. These schools offer short-term courses of a year or less and associate's, bachelor's, and master's degree programs. After any of these programs, a graduate can apply to the American Culinary Federation for one of its fourteen types of certification, each one demanding particular qualifications. Every certificate requires passing a written exam that shows the applicant's knowledge and a practical exam that demonstrates skills. The federation also offers apprenticeships that let budding chefs perfect their culinary techniques by working alongside experienced cooks and chefs.

The fourteen different culinary certifications illustrate the variety in this field. Chefs can specialize in pastries, sauces, soups, seafood, meats, or desserts. Cooks can be primarily grillers, fryers, bakers, short-order cooks, or fast-food cooks. Other kitchen workers can toss salads and cut and assemble ingredients for cold sandwiches. There are many culinary, nutrition assistant, and management positions in food service systems.

Chapter 5

Nutritional Counseling

ne of the most diverse areas in the dietetics and nutrition field is that of nutritional counseling. It includes dietitians, consultants, counselors, trainers, and coaches. People in this field work in clinics, offices, gyms, and private homes. They may have advanced degrees or no degree at all. Some work a typical forty-hour week and some are part-time. Their clients are young and old, sick and healthy, competitive athletes and the not so spry.

Private Nutritional Consultant

Some clinical dietitians prefer to work in private practice instead of in a hospital setting. They provide nutrition therapy to outpatients—patients who are not in hospitals—in their offices or the patients' homes. Sometimes doctors want their patients to work with a dietitian to get or keep their medical conditions under control. The doctors refer them to private-practice dietitians who work as consultants. The dietitians get the medical diagnosis and lab results from the doctors and ask the patients to write out a diary

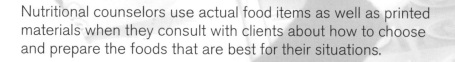

Nutritional counselors use actual food items as well as printed materials when they consult with clients about how to choose and prepare the foods that are best for their situations.

of what they have been eating. They analyze the patients' diet patterns and advise them about the best way to eat for their conditions. They meet with the patients as many times as it takes to help them develop good eating habits. They report their patients' progress to the doctors who referred them.

Some nutritional consultants specialize in managing certain chronic conditions. They may work in a private clinic that treats people with diabetes, high blood pressure, kidney disease, or weight problems—conditions that respond to nutrition therapy. They may develop specific programs for people with food allergies, eating disorders, or other dietary challenges.

Dietitians and nutritionists are concerned not only with people who are ill; they also help people stay fit. Many sports teams hire nutritional consultants, usually sports dietitians. The nutritional demands of professional athletes are different from those of people who are not as intensely active. Besides, teams travel and players often need help maintaining a healthy diet when they go to new places.

Business owners of all types are recognizing the importance of having fit employees. They know that healthier workers have better attitudes and are more productive. So leaders in several corporations hire nutritional consultants to help them create workplace environments that promote health. The consultants introduce better selections in the company cafeteria and vending machines. They write articles for the companies' newsletters and Web sites, post recipes and nutrition resources, provide nutrition classes, give food demonstrations, and offer one-on-one

A ROYAL JOB

Football, baseball, basketball, and hockey teams can all use nutritional counsel, and registered dietitian Mitzi Dulan has given her professional advice to teams in all four sports. Currently, she is the team nutritionist for the Kansas City Royals (baseball) and the Kansas City Chiefs (football). Her job combines education, personal counseling, and food management. At the beginning of the training season, Dulan makes presentations to the teams, explaining how to eat to be at their best, to boost their energy, and to recover from physically and emotionally exhausting games. When the teams are playing, she works with the clubhouse staff to make sure they provide foods that will keep the players fit and energized. Throughout the year, during the playing season and in the off-season, she meets with individual players, helping them set and work toward their personal fitness goals. She creates meal plans and finds personal chefs for some of the players. She is never "off duty." She often receives phone calls or texts from athletes who are at a restaurant or a grocery store and have questions about foods. She doesn't mind the calls; she loves her job. Besides, she has one great extra: good seats at all the games.

counseling to employees. Some consultants specialize in workplace nutrition.

Dietitians in private practice have two job challenges. In addition to being skilled in nutrition, they must also be good business people. Because they are in business for themselves, they have to do their own scheduling and billing, keep good records, and handle other office tasks. They often work on a contract basis; that is, they sign agreements with medical offices or companies to do work for them. That means they have to build relationships with doctors, health care facilities, and company executives so that they will refer clients to them.

Weight-Loss/Fitness Counselor

Private nutritional consultants are usually experts who have worked a number of years in the field. They usually have a bachelor's or master's degree in nutrition science or a related field. But there are counseling areas open to people with less than a four-year degree. Two very popular ones are weight-loss counselor and fitness trainer.

Some weight-loss counselors work in bariatric facilities—hospitals or clinics

that treat obesity. Some work in weight-loss centers or gyms. Others work for diet programs such as Weight Watchers, Nutrisystem, or Jenny Craig. Weight-loss counselors work with individual clients one-on-one or in small

Although this counselor works for a diet food company, he knows that good nutrition and exercise go hand in hand. He is conducting an event that teaches both diet and exercise.

groups. They generally have knowledge and experience not only in nutrition, but also in exercise science.

People who are concerned not only with their weight but also with their physical strength and stamina sometimes seek the help of a fitness counselor or personal trainer. Fitness counselors work in gyms, hospitals, resorts, spas, and camps. They develop diet and exercise programs tailored to the needs, goals, and lifestyles of individual clients. They also help their clients stay motivated and work at reaching their fitness goals. That requires skills in psychology as well as exercise and nutrition.

Wellness Coach

Weight-loss and fitness counselors work with people with very specific goals: losing weight or improving fitness. Wellness coaches are concerned with the entire range of health issues: weight, fitness, disease prevention, and maintaining overall health. They are sometimes called lifestyle coaches or health coaches. They focus on the lifestyle choices people make that affect their health. Those choices involve eating, drinking, exercising, smoking, and sleeping. They include the ways people manage their time and how they handle stress. Wellness coaches help their clients replace bad habits with healthy ones.

As with other nutritional consultants, many wellness coaches are in business for themselves, working with individuals who have been referred to them. Some contract with companies that offer fitness, nutrition, and wellness services to their employees. Still others work for health insurance companies. Some health insurers are finding that wellness coaches can be very effective in helping people develop and stick with healthy habits. The healthy choices lead to healthy lifestyles, and the healthy lifestyles result in less illness and lower costs for the insurance companies.

Wellness coaching is a growing health care field and a good entry point for a person with some training in nutrition. It combines nutrition with fitness, psychology, teaching, counseling, and motivating. Being a wellness coach does not require any degree, but some people who hire coaches or refer people to them prefer that the coach have an associate's degree in nutrition science or a health-related field. A number of schools and online programs offer classes for people who want to become health coaches.

Holistic Counselor

All of the consultants described so far are conventional, or traditional, practitioners. Holistic nutritional counselors offer a different approach. They advise their clients on how to use herbs, vitamins, natural supplements, and detoxification as well as whole foods to achieve a healthy balance between body, mind, and spirit. Holistic nutrition counselors often combine, or integrate, the alternative perspective with conventional methods. They are called integrative nutrition counselors.

As with wellness coaching, traditional and online schools and organizations offer courses, degrees, and certifications in holistic nutrition. It is one of the many career paths in dietetics and nutrition that can be entered within two years of high school graduation.

Chapter 6

Careers in Business and Industry

People usually associate dietetics and nutrition with health care or culinary careers, but jobs are also available in other industries. Nutrition expertise is needed in businesses that manufacture or sell foods and beverages, in universities and institutes that do research on foods or dietary practices, and in government agencies that oversee a nation or state's food supply. Many jobs in these places are advanced positions, requiring at least a bachelor's degree. However, DTRs, people with two-year degrees, and students who are still in the education process can also find work in these areas.

Researcher and Product Developer

Research and product development go hand in hand. Food manufacturers are always looking for something new to offer customers. Because today's customers are more health-conscious than ever, food and drink companies want the new products to be nutritious. Research dietitians analyze ingredients, calculate amounts and

Dietitian Evelyn Tribole measures ingredients carefully. She uses her knowledge of nutrition to create cookbooks with easy, nutritious, and tasty recipes.

nutritional values, and test for taste. Researchers study food trends and experiment with combinations of colors and flavors.

What goes into a food product is only part of the food manufacturing industry. The way it is prepared and how it is packaged also affect the quality, cost, and appeal of a food item. Companies need people who can improve or develop safe and efficient processes for preparing their products. They need people who can create packaging that keeps food good for longer periods, protects it in

SUPERMARKET DIETITIAN

For most people, good nutrition starts at the grocery store, so that is where Barbara Ruhs works. As a dietitian, her passion is educating people about healthy food choices. She worked for a while in public health before switching to consulting. She decided the best way to help the most people make the wisest food selections was to go where they purchase their food: the supermarket.

Now Ruhs works for a large grocery chain. She figures out ways to interest the chain's customers in buying healthy products. One way is to invite them to sample items at display tables in the stores or at booths at community health events. Another is to conduct nutrition education tours of the stores for clubs and groups. Ruhs writes a nutrition newsletter every other month and a flyer with food recommendations and nutrition information that reaches millions of the chain's customers every week. She is also available to answer customers' questions. She has many titles: dietitian, product promoter, event planner, and public relations manager. Each job enables her to pursue her passion: making a difference in public health.

shipping, makes it look better, and is more environmentally friendly. For these tasks they hire food technologists and food technicians. Their degrees are not in nutrition or dietetics but in food science. Food technologists have bachelor's degrees or higher, and food technicians generally have associate's degrees. Often technologists and technicians work together. The technologists select and perform experiments, and the technicians assist by setting up equipment and recording results.

Some food research is not connected with commercial products. Government agencies and private institutes conduct studies to learn general information about how foods and eating patterns affect health. How much potassium should the average person consume? Does eating or drinking caffeine cause hyperactivity? How does salt affect blood pressure? Research dietitians design and conduct studies to answer questions like these.

Marketer and Promoter

The current interest in healthy eating has led companies that sell food to use dietitians and nutritionists in their promotions departments. Grocery and restaurant chains and food manufacturers want people to know how nutritious their food is. So do commodity groups such as the Dairy Council, Beef Commission, and Raisin Growers' Board. These large companies and groups hire dietitians to be their spokespeople, telling the public about the nutritional value of their offerings. The dietitians create advertisements, fact sheets, recipes, and other materials. They write the food labels that list the nutritional content of products and calculate how many calories are in the

Food companies sometimes provide community events on healthy eating that feature their products and use nutritionists as their spokespeople. This dietitian is conducting a back-to-school workshop promoting balanced nutrition.

foods on restaurant menus. They pen articles for magazines and blogs for their employers' Web sites. They might put together cookbooks with recipes that feature their companies' products. Corporate marketing positions of this type are nearly always filled by registered dietitians.

Other Positions

Registered dietitians are also the ones that food processing companies call on for quality control. Quality assurance managers see that the right ingredients are used in the proper amounts in all food products. They inspect the machinery and procedures used at every stage at which the food is handled. All must comply with the regulations and standards that govern their industry. Dietitians who perform quality control work for food companies, but many dietitians and nutritionists like the freedom of working on their own.

Some start their own businesses. Nutritionists, particularly holistic nutritionists, might open or manage health food stores. Some have health clubs or run fitness camps. Some create new products like nutrition supplements and promote those products. Some operate catering companies. Being in business for themselves gives them flexibility.

One job that offers great flexibility is freelance writing. With today's emphasis on healthy eating, people are eager for information on foods. They want to know how to cook new foods, how to make their favorite recipes healthier, what diets will help them lose weight, and what foods will lower their risk of certain diseases or boost their energy level or performance. For a person with some experience in a nutrition field and a flair for writing, freelancing can be a side job or a career path. There are many opportunities for nutrition writers. Cooking, health, and fitness magazines carry articles on nutrition. Professional journals publish research. Men's, women's, and parenting magazines are interested in foods. Travel

certifications, they can also move up the ladder and the pay scale to increasingly more responsible positions.

Preparing for a Career in Nutrition

Good job prospects usually mean strong competition for the positions. Choosing courses wisely and studying hard in high school can give students a jump on the competition. Nutrition is a science, so high school students interested in dietetics would be smart to take science courses. Biology and chemistry classes will provide a foundation for the tougher science programs that students will encounter in college. Health classes and math, particularly algebra, will also be helpful. Any classes that have to do with food, such as home economics, are good choices.

Most dietitians and nutritionists interact with people. Therefore, high school classes that help students understand others and communicate well, such as social studies, English, and psychology, are good preparation for a career in this field. Because many in the field go into private practice, taking business courses would be wise, too. People who are self-employed need to have computer skills, knowledge of accounting, and an understanding of how businesses work.

Involvement in extracurricular activities, such as sports, clubs, and volunteer service always gives students an edge over the competition. College admissions directors as well as employers like to see that students are busy doing something productive. High school teachers or counselors might be able to direct students to volunteer, internship, work experience, or other opportunities related

The understanding of chemistry these students are gaining in this science classroom is a solid foundation for a career in dietetics or nutrition.

to nutrition. These experiences give students a realistic view of some of the jobs that are available in the field.

While in high school, students can explore the different options that will be available to them upon graduation. Which kind of program best fits the student's career goals and financial situation? An associate's degree or a bachelor's degree program? A didactic program or a coordinated program? Dietitian or nutritionist? Conventional or holistic? If students opt for an associate's degree program

NUTRITION ENTREPRENEUR

Jenny Westerkamp believes in making things happen. When she discovered the nutrition field as a junior in college, she switched her major from biology to dietetics. She knew she needed a mentor to guide her through the maze of all the possible choices. She did an Internet search for dietitians in her area and came across the bio of Julie Burns. Burns had several professional athletes as clients, and Westerkamp liked the idea of sports nutrition. She e-mailed Burns and wrote in the subject line "I want your job." She was delighted when Burns agreed to become a mentor to her.

Burns let Westerkamp shadow her on the job and work with her during Westerkamp's summer break from school. She inspired her, introduced her to people, and encouraged her. When Westerkamp received her RD credential, Burns hired her part-time. She also fanned the flame of Westerkamp's entrepreneurial spirit. Westerkamp saw a need among dietetic students for resources, help finding internships, and career coaching. She began her own online business to fill that need. Today, she works as a full-time sports nutritionist at her mentor's company, manages the business she started, writes nutrition e-books, and serves as president of a food and nutrition network. She not only *believes* in making things happen; she actually *makes* things happen.

with a plan to go for a bachelor's degree later, will the lower-level classes be counted toward the higher degree? What high school classes are required for entry into the college program? Answering these questions will make students ready for the next step after high school graduation.

In School and on the Job

Once students get to college, much of their time must be devoted to studying. But some energy also has to be spent exploring—getting to know the many aspects of the field and the influential people in it. The field of dietetics and nutrition is so large that students need to take every opportunity to learn what is available. They can volunteer at a hospital, nursing home, clinic, or food bank. They can work in a food service system. Students can enroll in short-term programs during their school breaks and job shadow local dietitians. The more they know about the different career paths, the better able they are to decide which avenue feels right for them. Plus, every activity they pursue is an experience that makes their résumé stand out when they look for employment.

High schools used to have home economics classes that taught students a little about cooking; today's high schools prepare students for jobs and careers in the health care and food industries.

The different experiences give them chances to meet people. In nutrition, as in many professions, getting a job is all about relationships. Even landing an internship, a requirement for RD credentialing, often takes a connection. Advancing in the profession and getting referrals come through knowing the right people. Often students and practicing dictitians and nutritionists have to find the right people.

One way to find the people who can help further a career is to network. All kinds of nutritionists attend professional conferences. Conferences are great places to meet others, learn what is new or hot in the field, and explore the many shades of the profession. Joining professional associations is another way to make connections. The Academy of Nutrition and Dietetics lists more than twenty-five

Gatherings such as this annual meeting of the School Nutrition Association are opportunities to learn and sample what is new in the field and meet people who might serve as mentors.

practice groups precisely for the purpose of providing networking opportunities. Each group is made up of professionals involved in a specific area of nutrition practice, such as behavioral health, infectious disease, vegetarian nutrition, and women's health.

Any one of these contacts can be doubly valuable as a mentor. Having a mentor in college and in the early stages of practice is one of the best ways of guaranteeing success in pursuing a career. Mentors serve as guides, teachers, examples, and encouragers. They open doors and help people become established. Having a good mentor makes finding a job and moving up in it much easier.

After they have practiced for a while, many dietitians and nutritionists are happy to become mentors because they enjoy their jobs. Many are passionate about helping others learn how to eat and live well. Whether they are in clinical practice, community nutrition, or food service, they know they are contributing to the health of their communities. They are treating diseases; educating people; and preparing wholesome, safe, and delicious foods. They are serving in careers that make their world a better place.

GLOSSARY

acute Serious, sharp, or severe. In medical usage, acute refers to a condition that is short-term, that may appear quickly, and that progresses rapidly.

bariatrics The branch of medicine concerned with the causes and treatment of obesity.

chronic Lasting a long time or recurring frequently, often becoming more serious as time goes on.

clinical Having to do with observing and treating patients who are sick.

commodity group A trade association of companies or individuals involved in the production and sale of a particular type of good, such as dairy products, corn, or poultry.

culinary Related to a kitchen or cooking.

detoxification The process of removing toxins (poisons) or other harmful substances from the body.

holistic Related to the whole or complete system, rather than parts of a system. Holistic nutrition focuses on using natural foods to achieve physical, emotional, and spiritual health.

nutrient A substance taken into the body that is necessary for growth and life.

physiology The branch of biology concerned with the ways that living things and their parts function.

practitioner A person who practices, or performs the tasks of, a particular profession.

Academy of Nutrition and Dietetics
120 South Riverside Plaza, Suite 2000
Chicago, IL 60606-6995
(800) 877-1600
Web site: http://www.eatright.org
Formerly the American Dietetic Association, the Academy of
   Nutrition and Dietetics is the world's largest organization
   of food and nutrition professionals. Its goal is to improve
   the nation's health and promote the profession of dietetics
   through education, research, and advocacy. It accredits
   training programs for nutrition professionals, credentials
   dietitians and nutritionists, and provides information to the
   public on a wide range of topics concerning food,
   nutrition, and healthy living.

American Culinary Federation
180 Center Place Way
St. Augustine, FL 32095
(800) 624-9458 or (904) 824-4468
Web site: http://www.acfchefs.org
The American Culinary Federation is a national organization
   of cooks and chefs that provides educational resources,
   training, apprenticeships, and certification to chefs. It also
   puts on events and puts out publications that promote the
   profession.

American Society for Nutrition
9650 Rockville Pike
Bethesda, MD 20814
(301) 634-7050

Web site: http://www.nutrition.org
The American Society for Nutrition is an association of
health and medical professionals and students that
advances nutrition research and practice through
publications, education, and programs.

Association of Nutrition and Foodservice Professionals
406 Surrey Woods Drive
St. Charles, IL 60174
(800) 323-1908
Web site: http://www.ANFPonline.org
The Association of Nutrition and Foodservice Professionals is
a national nonprofit association of food service professionals. It sets standards for the industry and provides its
members with career development resources, certifications, education, and resources.

Canadian Nutrition Society
310-2175 Sheppard Avenue East
Toronto, ON M2J 1W8
Canada
(888) 414-7188 or (416) 491-7188
Web site: http://www.cns-scn.ca
Formed in 2010, when the Canadian Society for
Clinical Nutrition merged with the Canadian Society
for Nutritional Sciences, the Canadian Nutrition
Society promotes the study and practice of nutrition
science and education.

Center for Nutrition Policy and Promotion
3101 Park Center Drive, 10th Floor
Alexandria, VA 22302-1594

(703) 305-7600
Web site: http://www.cnpp.usda.gov
A division of the U.S. Department of Agriculture, the
    Center for Nutrition Policy and Promotion develops
    and publishes dietary guidelines and other materials
    that help the public maintain good nutrition.

Dietitians of Canada
480 University Avenue, Suite 604
Toronto, ON M5G 1V2
Canada
(416) 596-0857
Web site: http://www.dietitians.ca
Dietitians of Canada is a professional organization of dieti-
    tians committed to advancing the health of Canada's
    citizens through food and nutrition. It accredits training
    programs and provides materials and information about
    food and nutrition through a public Web site.

National Society of Health Coaches
269 Lakeview Way
Winchester, TN 37398
(866) 916-6742
Web site: http://www.nshcoa.com
The National Society of Health Coaches, established in
    2007, provides certification, information, and
    resources for professional wellness coaches.

Society for Nutrition Education and Behavior
9100 Purdue Road, Suite 200
Indianapolis, IN 46268
(800) 235-6690 or (317) 328-4627

Web site: http://www.snbe.org
This association of professionals is involved in nutrition
    education and health promotion. In addition to provid-
    ing resources to its members, the society offers
    information and resources to the general public.

U.S. Bureau of Labor Statistics
Postal Square Building
2 Massachusetts Avenue NE
Washington, DC 20212
(202) 691-5200
Web site: http://www.bls.gov
An agency within the U.S. Department of Labor, the Bureau
    of Labor Statistics is responsible for calculating labor
    market activity, working conditions, and price changes in
    the U.S. economy. It provides essential information about
    the U.S. workforce and careers in its Occupational
    Outlook Handbook, including for dietitians and nutrition-
    ists (http://www.bls.gov/ooh/Health care/Dietitians
    -and-nutritionists.htm).

Web Sites

Due to the changing nature of Internet links, Rosen
Publishing has developed an online list of Web sites
related to the subject of this book. This site is updated
regularly. Please use this link to access the list:

http://www.rosenlinks.com/HCC/Diet

FOR FURTHER READING

Bickerstaff, Linda. *Careers in Nutrition*. New York, NY: Rosen Publishing, 2008.

Chalmers, Irena. *Food Jobs: 150 Great Jobs for Culinary Students, Career Changers, and Food Lovers*. New York, NY: Beaufort Books, 2008.

Echaore-McDavid, Susan, and Richard A. McDavid. *Career Opportunities in Agriculture, Food, and Natural Resources*. Chicago, IL: Ferguson, 2010.

Edmund, Steve. *Eating for Energy*. Bloomington, IN: Author House, 2011.

Ferguson Publishing. *Coaches and Fitness Professionals*. Chicago, IL: Ferguson, 2008.

Ferguson Publishing. *Medical Technicians and Technologists*. Chicago, IL: Ferguson, 2009.

Greenleaf, Barbara. *Good-to-Go Café*. Santa Barbara, CA: More Mesa Press, 2011.

Hill, Kathleen Thompson. *Career Opportunities in the Food and Beverage Industry*. Chicago, IL: Ferguson, 2010.

Hinton, Kerry. *Cool Careers Without College for People Who Love Food*. New York, NY: Rosen Publishing, 2009.

Kessler, David A. *Your Food Is Fooling You: How Your Brain Is Hijacked by Sugar, Fat, and Salt*. New York, NY: Roaring Brook Press, 2013.

La Bella, Laura. *Dream Jobs in Sports Fitness and Medicine*. New York, NY: Rosen Publishing, 2012.

Meyer, Susan. *A Career as a Chef*. New York, NY: Rosen Publishing, 2012.

Payne-Palacio, June R., and Deborah D. Canter. *The Profession of Dietetics: A Team Approach*. 4th ed. Sudbury, MA: Jones and Bartlett Learning, 2011.

Shadix, Kyle W., D. Milton Stokes, and Jenna A. Bell. *Launching Your Dietetics Career.* Chicago, IL: Academy of Nutrition and Dietetics, 2012.

Smith, Scott M., Janis Davis-Street, Lisa Neasbitt, and Sara R. Zwart. *Space Nutrition.* Bloomington, IN: Trafford, 2012.

Smith, Terry L. *Nutrition and Food Safety.* New York, NY: Chelsea House Publishers, 2010.

Smolin, Lori A., and Mary B. Grosvenor. *Nutrition and Eating Disorders.* New York, NY: Chelsea House Publishers, 2010.

Traster, Daniel. *Welcome to Culinary School: A Culinary Student Survival Guide.* Upper Saddle River, NJ: Prentice Hall, 2009.

Westerkamp, Jenny. *Getting Matched: A Guide for Dietetic Students.* All Access Internships, 2011. E-book available at http://www.allaccessinternships.com/GettingMatched.AGuideforDieteticsStudents.pdf.

Winterfeldt, Esther A., Margaret L. Bogle, and Lea L. Ebro. *Dietetics: Practice and Future Trends.* 3rd ed. Sudbury, MA: Jones and Bartlett Learning, 2010.

BIBLIOGRAPHY

Academy of Nutrition and Dietetics. "Become an RD or DTR." Retrieved January 8, 2013 (http://www.eatright.org/BecomeanRDorDTR).

Academy of Nutrition and Dietetics. "History." Retrieved January 4, 2013 (http://www.eatright.org/about/content.aspx?id=8487).

CityTown Info. "Career Story: Community Nutritionist Working with Disadvantaged Women and Children." Retrieved January 4, 2013 (http://www.citytowninfo.com/career-story/dietitians-and-nutritionists/community-nutritionist-working-with-disadvantaged-women-and-children).

Job Shadow. "Interview with a Dietetic Technician." Retrieved December 27, 2012 (http://www.jobshadow.com/interview-with-a-dietetic-technician).

Koszyk, Sarah. "Dietetic Career Spotlight: Jenny Westerkamp, RD." *Nutrition Jobs*, November 17, 2011. Retrieved January 4, 2013 (http://www.nutritionjobs.com/blog/blog/dietetic-career-spotlight-jenny-westercamp-rd).

National Food Service Management Institute. *A Guide to Centralized Food Service Systems*. University, MS: National Food Service Management Institute, 2002.

Rashed, Soha. *Assessment of Nutritional Status*. Alexandria, Egypt: Alexandria University, 2009. Retrieved January 9, 2013 (http://www.slideshare.net/soharashed/assessment-of-nutritional-status).

Schaeffer, Juliann. "Field of Dreams." *Today's Dietitian*, September 2010, Vol. 12, No. 9, p. 26.

Sedgwick, Tali. "Nutrition Jobs' Dietetic Career Spotlight Interview: Barbara Ruhs, MS, RD, LDN, Corporate Dietitian for Bashas' Grocery Stores." *Nutrition Jobs*, December 1, 2010. Retrieved January 4, 2013 (http://www.nutritionjobs.com/blog/blog/career -path-spotlight/nutritionjobss-dietetic-career-spotlight -interview-barbara-ruhs-ms-rd-ldn-corporate-dietitian-for -bashas-grocery-stores).

Sedgwick, Tali. "Nutrition Jobs' Dietetic Career Spotlight Interview: Marie Miller, DTR." *Nutrition Jobs*, October 1, 2010. Retrieved January 4, 2013 (http://www .nutritionjobs.com/blog/blog/career-path-spotlight/ nutritionjobss-dietetic-career-spotlight-interview-marie -miller-dtr).

U.S. Department of Labor, Bureau of Labor Statistics. "Dietitians and Nutritionists." *Occupational Outlook Handbook*. Retrieved December 14, 2012 (http:// www.bls.gov/ooh/Health care/Dietitians-and -nutritionists.htm).

INDEX

About the Author

Ann Byers is an author, editor, and youth worker. She has conducted seminars on job search skills for teenagers and adults, organized career exploration events for young people, and created a job club to help inner-city youths develop employability skills. She lives in Fresno, California.

Photo Credits

Cover (figure) iStockphoto/Thinkstock; cover background and interior pages (food) eskymaks/Shutterstock.com; cover, back cover, p. 1 (background pattern) HunThomas/Shutterstock.com; pp. 4–5 (background) sfam_photo/Shutterstock.com; pp. 5 (inset), 20–21 © Edward Linsmier/Tampa Bay Times/ZUMA Press; pp. 8–9, 15, 23, 24, 32–33, 37, 64–65, 66 © AP Images; p. 17 Kallista Images/Getty Images; p. 27 Monterey Herald/ZUMA Press; p. 30 Sacramento Bee/ZUMA Press; p. 36 U.S. Navy photo by Mass Communication Specialist 2nd Class Andrea Perez; p. 39 Schweinepriester/Shutterstock.com; p. 42 © Meghan McCarthy/Palm Beach Post/ZUMA Press; p. 45 Burger/Phanie/SuperStock; pp. 48–49 AP Images for Jenny Craig; p. 53 © The Orange County Register/ZUMA Press; p. 56 AP Images for Edelmen PR; p. 61 Jon Feingersh/Blend Images/Getty Images.

Designer: Michael Moy; Editor: Kathy Kuhtz Campbell; Photo Researcher: Karen Huang